Watch It Grow

Backyard Life Cycles

Barbara Reid

North Winds Press
An Imprint of Scholastic Canada Ltd.

A seed, an acorn, tiny eggs in a pond or under a leaf: what do they have in common? They are all living things — like you! Each starts out small and goes through changes as it grows to become a flower, a tree, a frog or a butterfly.

For a monarch butterfly this transformation happens over a few weeks, while an oak tree may keep growing for more than a hundred years. A tadpole lives underwater but begins to breathe air when it becomes a frog. The leaves of a sunflower turn sunshine into food to help the plant grow.

Both scientists and artists are inspired by what they see in nature. They ask questions and make observations. The plants and animals in this book can be found in the countryside, parks or even city backyards. Learning about them may inspire you to go outdoors and look for them where you live.

What's growing in *your* neighbourhood?

Contents

Watch the monarch butterfly grow!

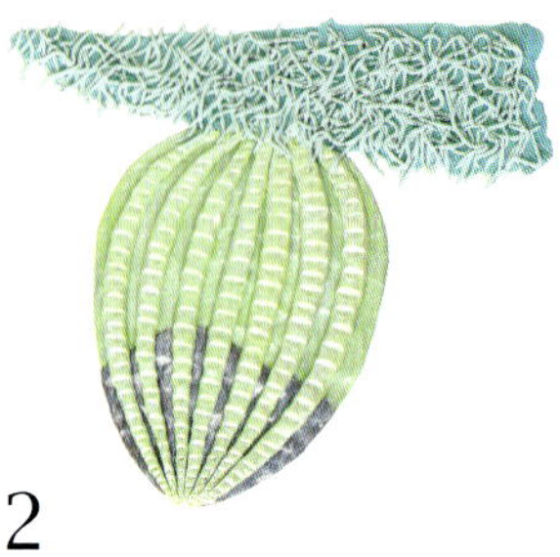

The monarch butterfly lays its tiny eggs on the bottom of a milkweed leaf. After four days, the egg hatches and out comes a caterpillar.

The caterpillar eats milkweed leaves and grows very quickly. Soon its skin gets too tight. The old skin splits open and falls off.

In two weeks, the caterpillar is five centimetres long. It spins a silk button so it can hang upside down.

The caterpillar splits its skin one last time, and reveals a chrysalis. Over the next two weeks, a butterfly will grow inside.

When the butterfly crawls out of the chrysalis, it dries itself in the warm sun. Then it unfolds its wings and takes flight.

The beautiful monarch butterfly flies from flower to flower, sipping nectar through its tubelike tongue.

Watch the sunflower grow!

The sunflower grows from a little seed.
The seed has a hard shell to protect it from
the cold winter.

The spring rain makes the seed split open. The root pushes into the earth and brings water to the growing stem.

The roots and stem grow quickly. In a few days, there are two leaves. They turn sunshine into food for the plant.

The stem grows straight up. Soon there are more and more leaves. A big flower bud forms on the top of the plant.

By the end of the summer, the plant is very tall. The bright yellow flower turns to follow the sun across the sky.

In fall, the plant dies and droops, heavy with seeds. Birds and squirrels will eat most of the seeds. But some will stay hidden under the ground. Next year, they will grow into more big, beautiful sunflowers.

Watch the green frog grow!

The green frog lays many eggs together in a mass of jelly. The jelly protects the eggs and keeps them warm under the cold spring water.

In a few days, the tiny tadpole hatches.
It lives underwater and attaches itself
to the plants it finds there.

The tadpole grows quickly. It begins
to swim around and to eat plants.

By the time it is eight weeks old,
the tadpole has sprouted back legs.
Now it gulps air from the surface of
the water and eats tiny bugs.

The tadpole's mouth and eyes get bigger, and its tail shrinks. It still lives underwater, but now front legs are beginning to grow.

Soon the small frog is ready to live on land, just like the big green frogs.

Watch the white oak grow!

The tiny acorn grows all summer long.
It turns brown as it ripens.

In autumn, the acorn falls to the ground. It stays buried under leaves and snow all winter. When spring comes, the acorn swells, and a white root pushes into the ground.

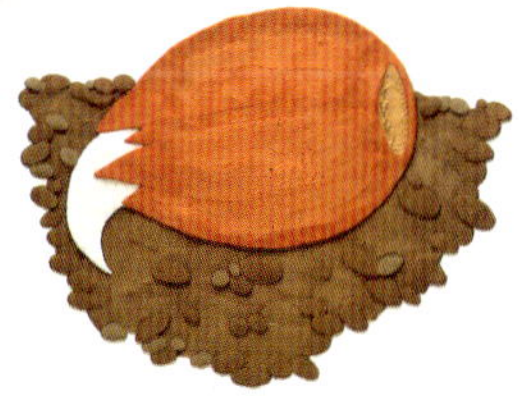

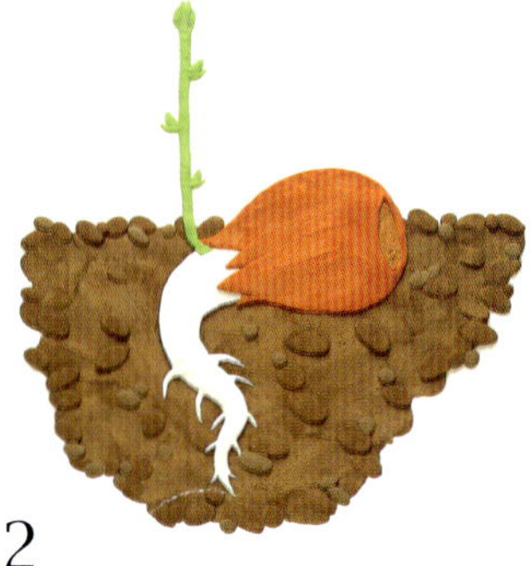

Soon a shoot grows straight up. It gets food from inside the acorn shell. It gets water from the root in the ground.

Next the tiny oak tree grows leaves. Now it is called a seedling. Under the ground, the seedling's roots spread and grow.

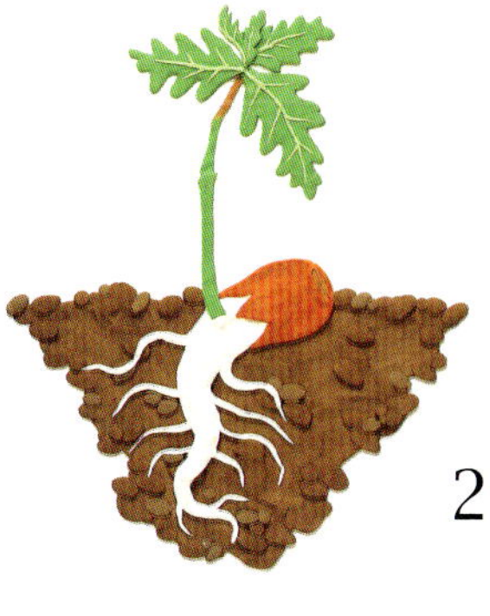

When the tree gets bigger, it is called a sapling. The sapling grows taller each year. Its trunk gets thick and woody and brown.

The oak tree grows and grows, and gets bigger and bigger. When it is fifty years old, it starts to make acorns. The magnificent oak tree may live hundreds of years.

Life cycle of the monarch butterfly

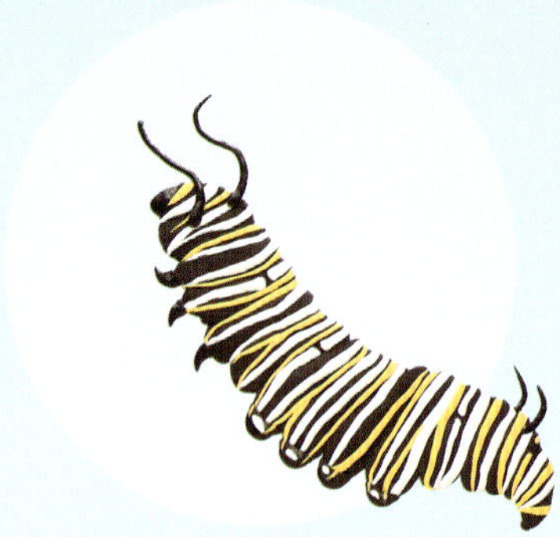

A caterpillar hatches from the egg

It spins silk to attach itself to a leaf

The butterfly lays its eggs on a milkweed leaf

It becomes a chrysalis and the butterfly grows inside

The butterfly emerges two weeks later

The butterfly flies

Life cycle of the sunflower

A seed waits through the winter

In the spring, the seed takes root

The roots and stem grow

A bud develops

It blooms into a large yellow flower

In the fall, the sunflower dies and its seeds drop

Life cycle of the green frog

The green frog lays its eggs in water

In a few days a tadpole hatches

The tadpole begins to swim and eat plants

The tadpole's legs develop and its tail shrinks

The froglet is almost ready to leave the water

The adult green frog lives on land

Lifecycle of the white oak

An acorn falls to the ground

In the spring, the acorn takes root

A tiny shoot begins to reach upward

The seedling grows, above and below ground

The sapling grows taller each year

After fifty years, the oak tree makes acorns

For Ernest
B.R.

Library and Archives Canada Cataloguing in Publication

Title: Watch it grow : backyard life cycles / Barbara Reid.

Names: Reid, Barbara, 1957- author, illustrator.
Identifiers: Canadiana 2019151846 | ISBN 9781443175593 (hardcover)

Subjects: LCSH: Animal life cycles—Juvenile literature. | LCSH: Plant life cycles—Juvenile literature.

Classification: LCC QH501 .R45 2020 | DDC j571.8—dc23

www.scholastic.ca

Photography by Ian Crysler.

6 5 4 3 2 Printed in Malaysia 108 20 21 22 23 24